WONDER
STARTERS

Eggs

Pictures by ESME EVE

Published by WONDER BOOKS
A Division of Grosset & Dunlap, Inc.

51 Madison Avenue   New York, N.Y. 10010

About Wonder Starters

Wonder Starters are vocabulary controlled information books for young children. More than ninety per cent of the words in the text will be in the reading vocabulary of the vast majority of young readers. Word and sentence length have also been carefully controlled.

Key new words associated with the topic of each book are repeated with picture explanations in the Starters dictionary at the end. The dictionary can also be used as an index for teaching children to look things up.

Teachers and experts have been consulted on the content and accuracy of the books.

Published in the United States by Wonder Books, a Division of Grosset & Dunlap, Inc.

ISBN: 0-448-09661-7 (Trade Edition)
ISBN: 0-448-06381-6 (Library Edition)

Printed and bound in the United States.

I like eggs.
I am eating a boiled egg.

1

Daddy likes eggs, too.
He is eating a fried egg.
2

Mommy uses eggs to make cakes.
She uses eggs to make pancakes.

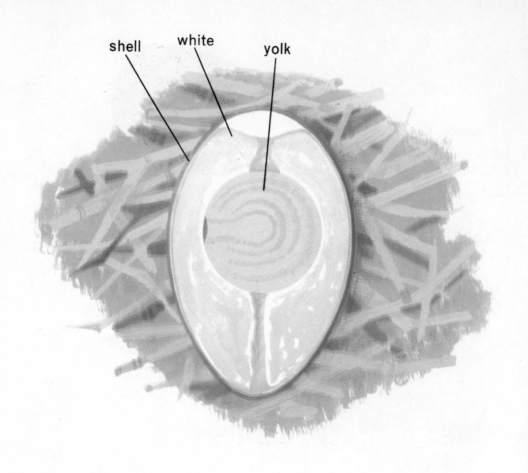

shell   white   yolk

Eggs have shells.
Inside the shell is the white
and the yolk.
The yolk is yellow.

4

The eggs most people eat
come from hens.
Some hens lay eggs every day.

5

The farmer takes the eggs away.
He sells the eggs.

On big farms hens live in coops.
They lay their eggs in boxes.

All birds lay eggs.
Most birds lay eggs in nests.
8

The mother bird sits on the eggs.
She keeps them warm.

9

A baby bird grows
inside the warm egg.
10

One day the baby bird hatches.
It breaks the shell with its beak.
It climbs out into the nest.

stork

eagle

weaverbird

woodpecker

pheasant

kingfisher

Some birds make nests in trees.
Some birds make nests in other places.
12

Other animals lay eggs.
Crocodiles lay eggs.
Some snakes lay eggs.

tortoise

butterfly

frog

snail

Frogs lay eggs.
Butterflies lay eggs.
Tortoises lay eggs.
Snails lay eggs.

14

Some animals eat eggs.
Rats steal eggs to eat.

Birds try to keep eggs safe.
Some birds make nests high in a tree.

Some birds lay eggs that are hard to see.
The colors help to hide the eggs.

Here is a sea bird's egg.
Look at the shape.
It does not roll into the sea.
It rolls around.

18

Big birds lay big eggs.
Ostriches lay the biggest eggs.

19

Long ago there were
animals called dinosaurs.
They laid very big eggs.

People have found dinosaurs' eggs
in rocks.
These are called fossils.
They are very old.

See for yourself
Make a sea bird's egg
out of putty or clay.
Make it this shape.
It will only roll around.
It will not roll straight.

22

cake
(page 3)

pancake
(page 3)

yolk
(page 4)

hen
(page 5)

farmer
(page 6)

nest
(page 8)

hatch
(page 11)

shell
(page 11)

beak
(page 11)

crocodile
(page 13)

snake
(page 13)

rat
(page 15)

butterfly
(page 14)

sea bird
(page 18)

tortoise
(page 14)

ostrich
(page 19)

snail
(page 14)

dinosaur
(page 20)

frog
(page 14)

fossil
(page 21)

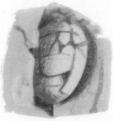